LONDON
Observed

LONDON
Observed

by
John Gay

commentary *by*
MACDONALD HASTINGS

THE JOHN DAY COMPANY, NEW YORK

Observing London's visitors, so readily identifiable as strangers always are in any country by that chain of office of the tourist, the camera, watching them posturing like temple dancers on the flagstones; weaving and twisting in search of new angles on old views, one may be excused for reflecting that London has been photographed too much already.

But then, just as you are dreading being brought face to face with another awful collection of holiday snapshots, an album turns up which is so fresh and exciting that it might be of a place which had never been photographed before. This is one of them.

Suddenly, Big Ben has a new and paternal expression on his dial. Lamp-posts have grace, people and traffic have shape, and cat-haunted alleys a beauty of their own. The teeming city is revealed as intimately as a village; or, rather, a conglomerate of villages.

The Cockney is surprised to discover how much his town he thinks he knows has changed in a decade under his own nose; the stranger how much more there is to see than the objects an uninterested courier points out through a motor-coach window.

London has never been an easy place for the occasional visitor to learn. She is an old lady who is traditionally punctiliously polite to her guests but, to people from more demonstrative cities, aloof. She expects the newcomer to cultivate her, not vice versa. She tries less than any capital I know to be liked. But to those who woo her patiently and persistently enough, hers is the warmest welcome of all.

John Gay has embraced London. He himself came here from Germany in the bad time for Europe twenty-five years ago. Today, he is a British citizen and a true Londoner of London's adoption.

I knew him first as a photographer of the English country scene, and learnt to admire the stark economy of detail with which he got his effects. It was later, when he showed me a portfolio of photographs of Hampstead, those northern heights of London where he has made his home, that I saw how sensitively he had lifted the misty veil which half hides London from herself.

This book is the achievement of two-and-a-half years in which, with the enthusiasm and understanding of a true lover, he set his lens to capture her heart. I believe that he has succeeded in a measure which only born Londoners have attained in the past.

John Gay isn't one of your photographers, like the tourists who stand at the end of the red carpet of the Mall, trying to fit in Buckingham Palace, the new skyscraper and, for all I know, the Wellington Barracks as well, in one exposure; not forgetting a London Bobby in the foreground. Gay's art is to establish how much he can leave out of his viewfinder, and still retain the impression in depth that an architectural elevation, a lump of old ironwork, or a puddle made on him.

Like John Betjeman, he loves street lamps, gnarled trees, chimney pots and buildings. But he instils such warmth and sense of period into them that none should need to be reminded that this is the city of Good Queen Bess and Queen Victoria; of Dickens and Cruikshank, Samuel Johnson and Samuel Pepys, William Hogarth and William Shakespeare, Palmerston and Gladstone; and, in a lighter context which is none the less enchanting, Nell Gwynne, Gilbert and Sullivan, and Peter Pan. Like John Ruskin in Venice, Gay sees London through her stones.

He rarely takes a colour photograph. When he does, as on the dust jacket of this book, it is always a model of disciplined colour control. Not for him the fruit salad of reds, yellows and blues of the seaside postcards. He prefers the aesthetic of black and white. The medium particularly suits this grey old city.

To amateur photographers who study this work, I commend Gay's brilliant feeling for the exact point of hardest focus. He uses it on his Rolleiflex like an index finger to point where he wants your maximum attention. His graphic comment is often unexpected. It seldom fails to be memorable.

But this book isn't primarily intended for the photographer although, since travellers are all photographers these days, it ought to be a help. Its other purpose is to introduce London in a frankly unconventional guide, intended for visitors with a taste for more than the Crown Jewels, the Hampton Court Maze, Brussels sprouts, warm beer, and Princess Margaret's new hair-do.

John Gay shows you some of the sights that please his own civilised outlook. In adding my personal comments, I have been careful to avoid giving the kind of information which you can acquire from an official guide book on any news-stand.

I have tried to say things about the anatomy of my native city which most visitors never hear; things which guides scarcely ever know. The introduction is in no sense definitive. London is too big and too old. Its outsides and its insides are too complex. Here is merely a beginning from which others, I hope, will make a private diagnosis of their own.

In his pictures, John Gay shows you some of the things which London has whispered to him. Taking my theme from his photographs, I have added what the pictures say to me.

MACDONALD HASTINGS

* * * * *Where better to start than the most exclusive address in the British Commonwealth? The Queen is at home in Buckingham Palace today. How do I know that? The answer is that, when she is in residence, her Royal Standard is flying from the pediment in the centre. In rough weather, it's a small flag known as 'the storm standard.' In ordinary conditions, the standard is rather larger. On state occasions, a magnificent piece of bunting is flown—red, blue and gold—which usually means that, before long, Her Majesty herself is likely to appear on the balcony.*

The Grand old Duke of York
He had ten thousand men.
He marched them up to the top of the hill
And he marched them down again.

There he is, the commander-in-chief whose ineptitude is immortalised in a nursery rhyme, looking down from his column on the band of the Irish Guards marching out of St. James's Palace, and the Household Cavalry on their way to mount guard on Horse Guards' Parade. From his perch overlooking the Mall, 'the grand old Duke' has small cause for complaint that times have changed. In their ceremonial uniforms, the Household Cavalry and the Brigade of Guards might be the same men whom, during a disastrous expedition in the Napoleonic Wars, he marched to the top of the hill and then marched down again.

A contemporary satirist, Harry Graham, wrote a song about the military pageantry which is part of London's pride. He called it 'The King's Horses and the King's Men':

They're not there to fight the foe,
You might think so, but oh dear no
They're there because they've got to go
To put a little pep into the Lord Mayor's Show.

It was a hit when it was written; but it was not, as the lyric writer well knew, quite fair. They look like toy soldiers in their bearskins, their plumed helmets and the kilt. But in battledress, their business wear, these same men are the shock troops, the élite of the British Army. In battle, they have unfailingly upheld the proud tradition that 'The Guards never duck!'

Turn the page, and observe the paradox of London only a few hundred yards behind His Grace's back.

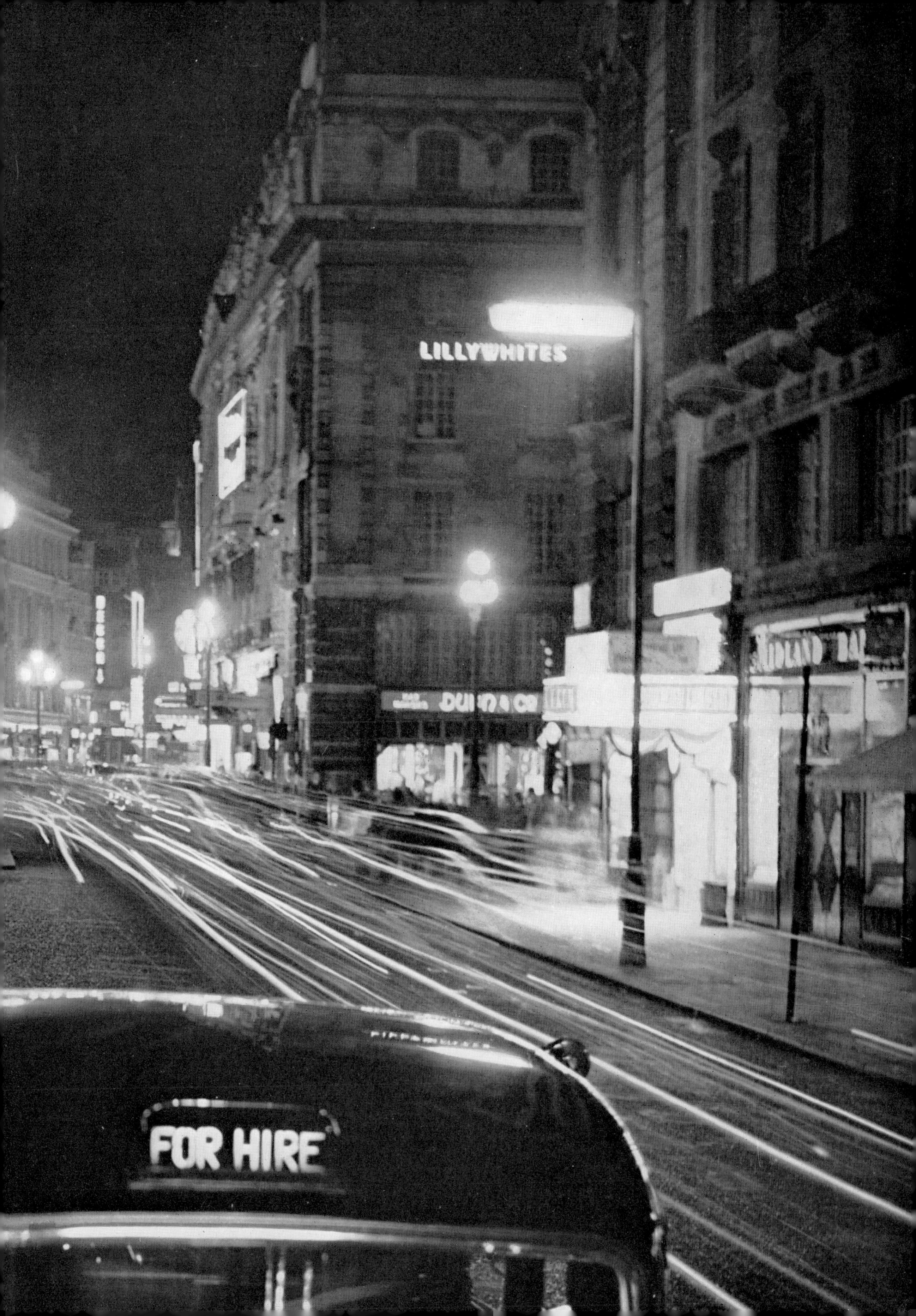
LILLYWHITES
FOR HIRE

That was Pic-
cadilly Circus
we've just passed,
and a good thing
because it was at a
time of night when
it is too noisy, and
too dangerous, by
half.

Surprisingly, this
is Piccadilly Circus
again, stilled by
John Gay in one of
those rare moments
which recall the
quiet elegance the
place used to have
when Eros first took
his stand in the
whirlpool; at a time,
in other days, when
it was often called
'The Centre of the
World.'

There's a saying
that you can't idle
for half an hour
in Piccadilly Circus
outside Swan and
Edgars within sight
of the magnificent
architectural sweep
of Regent Street
without meeting
somebody you
know. There's truth
in it.

But, ordinarily,
it's no place for a
poodle to cultivate
the acquaintance of
a pillar-box. It's an
obedient dog you
can trust off the
leash in what has
become the Times
Square of London.
There is little that's
elegant about it to-
day.

Those toy soldiers again—saluting the Queen in Hyde Park on the occasion of her official birthday. It's not really her birthday, but it suits London's convenience to celebrate every Sovereign's natal day on a fixed date (usually the first Sunday in June) in the optimistic hope that there will be many happy returns of sunny weather.

Characteristically, on the same day and in the same park, John Gay has photographed someone who has met his Waterloo. A hundred years ago, in Dickens's London, the down-and-out was an integral part of the pattern. Now, he is an anomaly, as rare on the streets as a horse-drawn carriage.

At the same time that Beau Brummel brought in the Englishman's starched neckcloth, his contemporary, John Nash, the architect, was clothing London in stucco. At the time, few people thought much of it:

Augustus at Rome was for building renown'd
And of marble he left what of brick he had found;
But is not our Nash, too, a very great master?—
He finds us all brick and he leaves us all plaster.

Nevertheless, John Nash achieved what Christopher Wren couldn't. After the Great Fire, Wren conceived a magnificent plan for a capital centred on the dome of St. Paul's. It remained a paper masterpiece. Nash, under the patronage of the Prince Regent, made a belated attempt to give a new character to the most planless city in the world. You can see his hand in columned terraces, usually painted yellow, all the way from Buckingham Palace to Regent's Park. This one, Cumberland Terrace, is the most extensive of them all.

On Nash's death in 1835, all that an obituary writer could bring himself to say of him was that 'as a speculative builder, this gentleman amassed a large fortune; but as an architect he did not achieve anything that will confer upon him a lasting reputation.' But he has. The buildings that came from Nash's drawing board are now generally regarded as part of London's pride. Anyhow, the best people still like living in them.

The unique characteristic which distinguishes London from all the other capitals of the Western world is that it is essentially a City of Men. Nowhere else will you find a masculine preserve comparable with the area which has its centre in St. James's. Although it is true that within recent years women have thrust a stiletto heel into the outer doors of clubland, the deepest sanctuaries, where the members snooze peacefully in leather-upholstered armchairs under the shelter of the *London Times*, still resist invasion.

About the clubs are the little shops which cater exclusively for masculine needs; his clothes, his pipes, his guns, his fishing tackle, his boots, his spurs, his umbrellas, and his hair-dos. They are shops which women seldom enter; shops in which the assistants are rather sacristans than salesmen; shops in which the price of things is only mentioned in whispers; shops which would regard the idea of advertising their wares with an icy shudder. They assume that anybody of taste knows their address and that they would rather cut their own throats than sell anything which was less than the best quality on earth.

I think it was Ed Murrow who went into one of the men's shops after the bombing of London, and remarked how pleased he was to find that it was still there. The assistant retorted stiffly: 'We've been here for two hundred years, sir.' I myself, trying on a hat one day, made the comment: 'It looks all right.' The hatter raised his eyebrows in polite surprise: 'If I may say so, it looks what it is, sir.'

London's repute as the male fashion centre dates from Regency times when Beau Brummell made his name synonymous with what a well-dressed man should be. Why the bulls of the bulldog breed are so fond of their worlds without women is arguable. Dr. Arnold, who invented the English public school system, is probably largely responsible. The clubs, where women are not admitted, could be described as an extension of schools like Rugby and Eton where only boys are allowed to go. Rightly or wrongly, the upper class English are still brought up in the tradition that women are all right in their proper place.

For a man, clubland is splendid.

The bow-fronted windows of Lock's in St. James's are part of it. The hats on display are all dusty antiquities of an earlier generation. You are supposed to know that Lock's aren't in the costumier's business, but one of the people who make the hats which are raised by the most elegant types about town.

The most famous clock in the world boomed the hour for the first time in 1860. Soon after it was built Big Ben, the great bell, cracked. Another, slightly smaller, was substituted. That one cracked as well. For several years afterwards, the hours were struck on one of the smaller quarter-hour bells; and then an expert suggested that the 16-ton Big Ben should be turned so as to present a new surface to the 1-ton hammer. This was done and Big Ben has gone on ever since. But people with musical ears can still discern that the chime has a crack in it.

It is a half-forgotten fragment of history that when the new Houses of Parliament were built—a group of buildings erected after the old ones had been burnt down and of whose beauty few Britons seem to possess a due consciousness—the original notion was to christen the clock Royal Victoria. It was named Big Ben, not without opposition, after Sir Benjamin Hall, First Commissioner of Works.

As a public timekeeper, Big Ben is the most accurate clock in the world, varying only a few seconds in a week. Oddly enough, it was the achievement not of a clockmaker but of a lawyer; a Mr. Denison who, with the Astronomer Royal, was appointed to provide the new Houses of Parliament with a time-piece. He wanted his machine not to vary more than one minute a week, which all horologers at the time declared impossible. But he invented a gravity escapement which even bettered the marvellous result he aimed for.

He achieved more than he dreamed. Who could have guessed in Victorian times that, in this century over the radio, the defiant voice of Big Ben would reassure the world in Britain's 'finest hour.'

Stop . . . The hand of the City policeman might be raised in warning
against Soho, the foreign colony locked
between the jaws of Shaftesbury Avenue
and Oxford Street. Depends where
you're heading for. Lining the narrow
crowded streets of Soho are some of the
best and most exclusive restaurants in
the West End of London. But inside
Soho, too, are the sleazy cafés where
reefers pass, and tired business men are
rooked to watch a strip tease. If you're
looking for trouble, you can find it here
in the dim dives of the underworld. If
you're after good food, Continental
delicacies, Cinerama, or real absinthe
filtered through loaf sugar, this is the
parish for you, too. Just check the
address before you walk in.

The name Soho is a relic of very
different times. 'So-ho' was the call of
the hunter when he viewed a hare
springing from her form. The game that
lurks in the shadows here now answers
another greeting.

It's a tribute to the political stability of the British, the national genius which recognises that there are two sides to every argument, that Whitehall, the seat of Government, has the statue of King Charles the First at the Trafalgar Square end and the man who chopped his head off, Oliver Cromwell, at the other. By way of analogy, just try and imagine statues of those old adversaries, Stalin and Krushchev, facing each other from their respective corners in Red Square.

John Gay's view is from Charles the First's corner with the equestrian statues of two Field Marshals in the referees's place in the middle.

Apart from the glittering spectacle of the soldiers of the Household Cavalry guarding Horse Guard's Parade, Whitehall is outwardly a relatively uninspiring street. But the visitor—the Londoner, too, because too few know about it—should take a look at the skyline made by the Ministries of This-and-That from the bridge which spans the lake in St. James's Park. From there, the enclave in which the civil servants stew up their buff forms and brew their tea looks like . . . well, a bit like the onion-domed Kremlin. And that's not so surprising as it might seem because, after all, the Kremlin's architect was a Scotsman.

For fiction-lovers, I have reason to suppose that James Bond's office isn't very far from here. The Admiralty, to which Captain Hornblower, R.N., brought so much credit, is just on the right of the road. The scaffold, under which the Three Musketeers and D'Artagnan hid in their frustrated attempt to save King Charles, was erected on this spot, too. Scotland Yard, whose detectives Sherlock Holmes held in such contempt, is at the end of the street on the left.

P.S. Contemporary 'Inspector Lestrades' who, in their own turn, haven't such a high opinion of Holmes's methods, are sometimes to be seen in a pub named after the prototype detective down Northumberland Avenue, which branches off Whitehall at the Trafalgar Square end. Holmes's addicts will like it.

PPS. Politicians, whom you can identify because the policeman on point duty at the end of Whitehall always hold up the traffic when they want to cross the road, roost inside the buildings over the page. The party exemplifying law and order on the outside are ornithologically described as black-headed gulls, although the adults have white heads. It is also of interest, for people who think that politics only concern humans, that the gulls on the Embankment refuse to have any contact with the gulls of the same species in St. James's Park over the road.

Every city has two faces, the humble and the proud. Here's the contrast; a row of terraced houses under snow in North London and (*right*) Nash's elevation of Carlton House Terrace overlooking the red carpet of the Mall. The one, ingrained with a hundred years of grime, a hangover of the Industrial Revolution when London sprawled into a maze of colourless streets with cynical names like Lavender Hill and Myrtle Road. The other a symbol of an Empire on which, according to Oscar Wilde, the sun would never set.

At the far end, von Ribbentrop, then the German Ambassador at the Court of St. James's, contrived the mischief which culminated in World War II. At this end, Charles de Gaulle strove under the Cross of Lorraine in the most desperate hour of France's history. In one of these mansions, George Nathaniel Curzon, 'a most superior person,' learnt that he would never be Prime Minister of England; and died in misery.

It's a daily event in any metropolis—the crowd of commuters from the dormitory towns and the suburb's emptying from the trains to fill the office blocks. Yet it's said that the scene in London differs in one respect from any other city in the world.

Look at the photographs carefully, and see if you can guess what it is. By way of a clue, the same comment has been made about Londoners, not only of our conduct on railway stations but of the manner with which we comport ourselves on our daily way everywhere.

It's something about us which defeats the foreigner like the extraordinary habit, among what in our newly classless society is called 'the lower income bracket,' of eating something out of a bag or a packet at every available opportunity. The English, even between meals, are forever munching.

Have you had enough time to resolve another enigma of the Anglo-Saxon temperament which is so indisputably revealed here? The answer is that London is the most unsmiling city in the world.

Compare what goes on here on the underground or any of the other great London termini, with the emotional explosion of laughter and tears which is as endemic as a train whistle on any railway station on the mainland of the Continent.

There's no moral. The Londoners' gloomy faces indicate neither happiness, nor the lack of it. It would be as unrealistic to draw conclusions from their faces as to imagine that people who snout about in paper bags are necessarily starving. It just happens that, facially, London is one of the most undemonstrative cities in the world.

From Monday to Friday, the square mile of the City of London mills with clerks and typists, brokers and commission men, top-hatted messengers, and over-nourished tycoons. At the week-end, it is relegated to the cats and care-takers. Here is Lombard Street while bankers are busy hitting golf balls into bunkers.

But, on the right, surely that isn't London? It *wasn't* until a very little while ago. Today, it's the view looking down from the very eye of London, the dome of St. Paul's. These are the office blocks, like piles of egg boxes, which have risen out of the rubble to which this area of the City was reduced in the London blitz. Sir Christopher Wren, 'who said to some men, if anyone calls say I'm designing St. Paul's' wouldn't, one fancies, have liked them one little bit.

'In these chambers, Madam, broken lives are as common as blackbirds.' The ruthless comment has been attributed to an eminent counsel asked to defend a lady in distress in the courts. His chambers might well have been here.

This is Middle Temple Lane, the entrance on the other side of Fleet Street from the Law Courts, to the advocates' domain. Here you may watch the lawyers, wigged and gowned, the judges looking only a little less awesome without their scarlet robes, proceeding down the narrow alleys into the village about the Temple Church where no wheeled traffic is permitted and black suits and striped trousers are the insignia that you belong.

It's an oddity of London life that Fleet Street, the home of newspapers, has at one end the Law Courts and the Temple and, at the other, the Central Criminal Court of the Old Bailey. It would seem difficult to imagine two estates more widely separated. Yet, just by Middle Temple Lane, almost within sound of the great underground presses of the popular papers, the professions of the law and of journalism socially unite in a club named, appropriately, 'The Wig and Pen.'

A national monument? A museum? Something to do with London University? Not a bit of it. True, this is a sort of national monument, and it's not far off from the University and the British Museum. You're in Russell Square in Bloomsbury, the area which is the traditional centre of book publishing (it published this one) and where long-haired intellectuals are reputed to use their baths to store their manuscripts.

But the people who flock into this apparently venerable building are only accidentally authors, or students, or curators. You're looking at the Imperial Hotel, as familiar a stopping-place for visitors to London as Euston Station just down the road. Underneath it is the famous Turkish bath, open day and, night, where overfed tycoons and underfed jockeys go to get their weight slapped off.

In the crazy drinks licensing system which prevails in this country, it is a piece of London lore that you can buy alcoholic refreshment, within the law, up to 2 a.m. in a restaurant with a licensing extension, and from 5 a.m. in the pubs in Covent Garden. You can drink all afternoon in the recognised clubs but, between two and seven in the morning, you are licked unless you are in a Royal Palace or a Turkish Bath. Ridiculous though it is, it is supposed to be part of the Turkish Bath treatment to drink after sweating it out in the steam room and under the hands of the masseur. Here is one place, which isn't a Royal Palace, where in the vaults they have a 24-hour licence.

It might be the setting for the climax of a Hitchcock thriller. It's the image of back-street London which, in imagination, is still typical. In fact, it's increasingly becoming an anomaly in the London, for better or worse, which is growing now.

The new American Embassy is only one contemporary new-comer. Skyscrapers have already arrived. In the past, the popular notion was that the London clay wouldn't carry skyscrapers. Now they're springing everywhere like dragon's teeth.

Although stovepipe buildings are dwarfing the ancient towers, steeples and spires, in isolation the old glory is undiminished. There are still quiet corners like the garden of Westminster Abbey where a boy can play cricket, and an old man remember a time when the green fields and the gardens stretched everywhere into London's heart.

With the growth of population, the countryside about London has been relentlessly pushed back. Only seventy-five years ago, you could drive to rural places in a pony trap from Piccadilly Circus. Today, it takes over an hour in a car.

The serenity of the past survives, but only just, in sanctuaries like this; its timeless beauty in old stones guarded by trees. The elevation overleaf is the Abbey.

It's a messy old skyline, a city which has spread the way it has through an age-long succession of compromises. London has grown through much the same series of accidents which laid an Empire in Britain's lap.

Nelson, whose victory at Trafalgar made Pax Britannica possible for a while, stands on his column on the right. The ball which crowns the London Coliseum at the bottom of St. Martin's Lane is on the left. The spire of St. Martin-in-the-Fields is left centre. But look at that majestic silhouette in the background.

At ground level, Westminster Abbey is smothered by so many other buildings that it is difficult to assess the length of the nave. But here you can see it in its true proportion.

The lesson of this picture for the stranger in London is never to try to find your way anywhere, least of all at the wheel of a car, without a map. The London streets are probably the most difficult in the world to unravel. When in trouble, remember that policemen all have street guides in their pockets. Cabbies, who have to pass a rigorous test on the geography of the metropolis before they can get a licence, have an encyclopaedic knowledge of the whereabouts of the most improbable addresses.

They're always 'ex-Service men.' They nearly all have 'a wife and children to support.'
And it's suspected that the pavement artists outside the National Gallery collect more
money than they will ever admit. Some of their work on the flagstones of London in
places where they are permitted a pitch, isn't, in its primitive way, too bad.

Every city has a façade; but, behind it, there's always another city lagging behind a hundred years or more. You've still only got to turn out of the main streets to find alleys like this. It depends on your own taste whether you find them evocative, romantic, or just sordid. This is a turning in theatre land, off St. Martin's Lane.

Every city has landmarks which identify it pictorially all over the world. Not necessarily the most beautiful, but rather the symbols of popular affection. Paris has the Eiffel Tower: New York the Statue of Liberty: Rome, the dome of St. Peter's. You'll think of others.

London, it seems to me, has four landmarks which identify it at a glance. Big Ben is the most familiar; but the outline of the dome of St. Paul's, or the dome of a London policeman's helmet, is all that any film director needs to identify the setting of his subject. Tower Bridge, the gateway to London, is the fourth.

Although the Tower of London, up river, is more ancient, although its toy fort outline is unforgettable, popular sentiment has chosen to associate the port of London with its Victorian suspension bridge rather than with the fortress which has guarded it for a thousand years.

The word London, so some people say, means place of the lakes. Before London was a city, the site was a marsh dotted with limpid pools and bracketed with slow-running streams. Part of the marsh, where St. James's Park is now, survived as late as the time of Henry VIII, and there were no less than eleven ponds during the reign of James I. The land about the Serpentine in Hyde Park is said to have cupped a lake since prehistoric times. But everybody in London has forgotten about London's origins—except the wild creatures.

For although a city of ten million people has grown out of the marshlands, although the lakes are now confined with concrete to a few small mirrors in the grey waste of central London, the instinct of the wild duck still guides them unerringly to their ancient flighting grounds. To this day, the wildfowl come up the Estuary from the sea and settle down to feed and rest in the heart of London.

It's a memorable phenomenon. But not more remarkable than the birds' adaptability to the ways of civilisation. Down river, they're still so wild that it needs a clever gunner to get within shot of them. But the moment they arrive in St. James's Park, they're so tame that they eat out of the Londoner's hands.

As far back as the fifteenth century, Londoners used to remark on the oddity. And in James the First's time it was decided to put it to good account. The king stocked the lake with fish and tame waterfowl, and improved the park with walks and fountains. By the time Charles II was perambulating with his spaniels on the banks, the St. James's Park lake was already a waterfowl sanctuary. The Restoration diarist, Evelyn, records that it was 'stocked with numerous flocks of several sorts of ordinary and extraordinary wildfowl breeding about one decoy which, for being so near a city and among such a concourse of soldiers and people, is a singular and diverting thing.'

Thus it is, deep in the heart of London today. The majority of the fowl are visitors; chiefly mallard, tufted duck and pochard. The rest are rare and foreign species of waterfowl which have been introduced at various times to the collection.

The lake in St. James's Park is preserved as a sanctuary for the waterfowl. Dogs must be kept on leads in the precincts, and boating is strictly limited.

The Serpentine is the human playground, and it must be one of the hardest worked stretches of water on earth.

Its surface is constantly stirring with the oars of pleasure skiffs, its boundaries lined with optimistic anglers. And, in an enclosure in the middle, it seethes in fine weather with bathers. And not only in fine weather.

If you get up early enough, one of the sights of the town is to see the hardy types who swim here every morning, summer and winter, on their way to work; even when they have to break the ice to do it. Most of them indulge in physical jerks, and take a run round the lake as well.

Oddly enough, the bathing enclosure is a comparatively recent innovation. It wasn't set aside for the purpose until the Minister of Works in the first Labour Government, George Lansbury, decided that London's lake could be put to better use. As the consequence, the little beach on the Serpentine has been called 'Lansbury's Lido' ever since. While it is still crowded during hot spells, it is not frequented as much as it used to be in less prosperous times.

Today, when almost every family has a car, the Londoners migrate to the sea. The parks are rather places for people exercising their dogs, nannies pushing perambulators, and lunch-time sandwiches.

The stranger will almost certainly notice how popular they are with loving couples, too. In this otherwise reserved city, the abandoned behaviour of Londoners lying on the grass often occasions raised eyebrows. But the Londoners themselves seem not to notice it; or, at any rate, they're content to mind their own business.

With all its homely charms, the English pub is ringed with anomalies and outmoded regulations. One of them, which is properly and widely disregarded in country districts, is that children are not allowed inside. So you can still see children like waifs waiting on the doorsteps while their parents are drinking at the bar.

It's a hangover from the reforming zeal of the Victorians when children needed protection to an extent that is not necessary now, when people in pubs were less well-conducted, and the gin palace spelt 'Mother's ruin.'

The habit of standing at bars, still divided into social classifications, is too ingrained a habit for the English ever to accept the Continental café system in which the whole family sits round the same table. But, lately, there has been a welcome tendency in pubs to provide rooms for children. These days, a lot of pubs sell sweets.

PS. If you wonder why pubs all have the colourful inn-signs they have, the tradition dates from the time when most people couldn't read. It was the picture on the sign which identified the place as 'The Red Lion,' 'The Green Dragon' and all the rest of the places which, in England, are the ordinary man's clubs.

The status symbols of our own time are a 'Jag' for Daddy, a 'mink' for Mummy, a 'hi-fi' for junior, and a pony for the pony-tailed daughter. This herd of fallow deer in Richmond Park are left over from a time when, in England, they were the greatest status symbol a man could have.

You'll find them in noblemen's parks about the country to this day. They are a damned nuisance to their owners because they are always breaking out into unwelcome territory. They are an expense because they require rangers to look after them; and they are unrewarding because venison, these days, is a flesh which is altogether too dry and black for palates educated to eat the cottonwool called 'a broiler.' Why bother to preserve them?

The answer is that the deer parks are one of the last survivals of feudal England when only the greatest in the land were permitted the right to harbour them; and when the poor serf risked having his hand chopped off, or worse, if he raised a bow and arrow to their fat flanks. Their proud antlers are a bit of English history which hasn't dropped off in its season. Latterly they have acquired a commercial value of a kind enough to make William the Conqueror turn in his grave.

The deer parks, where the privileged once exerted themselves in the art of venery, survive for the pleasure they give to week-end motorists on a picnic and the multitude who pay half-a-crown to trek round a stately home.

It is characteristic of the English that whenever they see an animal they want to feed it. It is precautionary to add that, in their season, stags are as dangerous as the rascals in castles who used to rule this land.

On the page behind lies 00° 00′, the Royal Naval College at Greenwich, the port down-river from which the map of the world is measured. In front of you is the memorial to Queen Victoria's consort and the dome of the Albert Hall named after him, erected in the ebullient age when London directed the affairs of an Empire which covered a fifth of the world.

The Albert Memorial has been laughed at in the past as a monument of bad taste. A wit made the comment that, after building a concert hall like a wedding cake, they ought properly to have placed the Albert Memorial as an ornament on the top of it. One good laugh would then have done for both of them.

But, contemporarily, Victoriana has its champions. The fussy arrogance of the Albert Memorial among the old trees of Kensington Gardens has come to be appreciated. There would be a helluva row if anybody proposed moving it. . . .

. . . and there would be one favourite subject the less for the snapshotters.

If there were nominations for a patron saint of tourism, Richard Boyle, Earl of Burlington, would surely appear on the short list. He was the high priest of the cult which, during the eighteenth century, made 'The Grand Tour of Europe' the fashionable thing to do; and the measure of its success the quantity of souvenirs the tourist brought back from his holidays.

Lord Burlington's villa at Chiswick belongs to an age when English noblemen vied with each other in bringing shiploads of art treasures from the Continent to house them in splendid mansions which harked back to the colonnaded style of the ancient architect Vitruvius, the sixteenth century Italian Palladio, and his disciple Inigo Jones.

He built his villa, not as a residence, but as a temple of art, a meeting-place where, surrounded by books and pictures, he could entertain the cultured world of his day. The poet Alexander Pope, who was a regular visitor, was so impressed by the taste of his noble patron that he dedicated to Lord Burlington the fourth of his Moral Essays, *Of the Use of Riches*.

When Lord Burlington built his villa, Chiswick was a rustic area within convenient distance of London. Today, Chiswick is just another metropolitan bus and underground route buried under a flyover. But the lovely Palladian-style building—John Gay reveals a tempting glimpse of it here—has been preserved.

Cutty Sark

The Thames is lined with hulks, from Captain Scott's *Discovery* to the tea-clipper, *Cutty Sark*. Deep down inside, we remain a nation of seagoers, as certainly as we are a nation of dog-lovers. Even now, when so much of Britain's merchant fleet is resting at its moorings, the mood is still there. One of the phenomena of more affluent times is that people with no conception of the size of an Atlantic swell—the old gentleman on the left knows all about it—are turning to small boats. At the drop of a hat, we would pioneer the sea again. Strand-on-the-Green.

Since it's murky on the facing page, a note concerning the English climate. Contrary to the popularly-held fallacy that London is the city of fog, the fact of the matter is that thanks to smoke abatement schemes 'a London particular' is now as rare as a hansom cab. Currently, the worst city in the world for smog is Los Angeles in sunny California.

Of course, it rains in London. In the time of the Roman occupation of these misty islands, Tacitus in his Natural History remarked on 'the constant moisture of the atmosphere and the dampness of the soil, which affords neither the vine, the olive, nor the fruits of warmer climates.' What he overlooked was that our moist atmosphere is Britain's greatest single asset.

Let those from more torrid climates, which so often thirst for rain, perpend for a moment in this land of macintoshes, goloshes and umbrellas. It's because we have 'the gentle rain from Heaven' that our soil yields its lush green grass. It's because we have the grass that we grow the animals which have made us the stockmen of the world.

It's because of the kindly rain that our womenfolk have complexions which are the envy of their suntanned sisters.

As the water sluices through the gutters and down the drains, as you pull your coat collar tighter about your neck, and tread warily through the puddles, remember that England has grown great through the caress of rain.

I remember hearing a story, perhaps apocryphal, of the English rose who is now our Queen. I hope it's true because, if it is, she made a comment worthy of her own great-great-grandmother. It's said that, on a visit to Niagara Falls, the mayor said to her: 'You've got nothing like this in England, ma'am.' To which, the Princess Elizabeth as she then was, retorted: 'Thank you, Mr. Mayor, we like our England as it is.'

This is the way it often is. Don't grumble about it. Learn to taste the flavour of the rain in a piece of English beef; in green vegetables, providing they haven't been butchered in bad restaurants; and in the colour of lovely girls' skins.

Karl Marx, the father of Communism, is buried here in Highgate. He cooked up his doctrines, at the expense of the British taxpayer, in the Reading Room of the British Museum. It is a fair comment on what they are worth that the sort of society he wanted to destroy is the one which harboured him, and which now respects his bones. In London there is always room for the man you disagree with.

For the refugee, too. It is a Cockney joke that you need a visa on your passport to travel to Hampstead or Highgate —so like a village even today. It is one of London's glories that, throughout the centuries, and especially this one, she has stretched a welcoming hand to the persecuted, the displaced, the dispossessed, the rebels and the homeless. Karl Marx was only one. Lenin was another. It makes one wonder why on earth the Russians have felt the need in Berlin to build a wall. Or does it?

Pond Square, Highgate

Londoners are accustomed to rain. But we so seldom have a heavy fall of snow that, when it comes, it's enough to make any Canadian, never mind a Muscovite, laugh till it hurts.

A few inches of snow like this makes front page news in the papers. The public transport system is dislocated. Private motorists get stuck. And the Ministry of Transport, the Royal Automobile Club and the Automobile Association issue solemn warnings on the state of the roads.

London is never prepared for snow. Commuters, with a frozen hard excuse for clocking in late, boast when they get to work as if they had crossed the Antarctic. The BBC encourages everybody to stay calm and, with a stiff upper lip, keep the wheels turning.

The London County Council hires casual workers with spades to disperse, very casually, shovelfuls of grit. The police, as always, are splendid. But London, which defied Hitler's blitz, has never learnt how to deal with a few flakes of snow.

Charles Dickens dreamed the white Christmas. The fact of the matter is that Christmas in Britain is usually just muggy and wet. The hard weather, if it comes at all, normally arrives later. In the years when it does, England is always caught by surprise.

Londoners treasure the memory of Frost Fairs in the past when oxen were roasted whole on the frozen Thames. The climate, owing to the recession of Arctic glaciers, may have changed a little since then. But the reason that there are no Frost Fairs now is more likely because, since the Embankment was built, London's river flows more swiftly.

In the snow, we are softies.

Hollybush Hill, Hampstead

The British Museum, a store of treasures inadequately housed, is always good for a letter to *The Times*. It is undeniable that, in the presentation of its incomparable collection, it doesn't compare with museums in the United States and many on the Continent. But we're getting better. The marbles which Lord Elgin brought from the Acropolis, and which the Greeks want back, are now well displayed.

Another cause for complaint is the loss of art treasures, mostly to the New World, in the auctions of private collections at Sotheby's. But the supply shows no signs yet of dwindling. What is hidden from the public gaze in Britain is still far larger than the exhibitions in the national museums and galleries.

P.S. The treasure isn't only in objets d'art. If you have a taste for looking at them, the London Parks and open places offer their own reward. It's said, for example, that the magnificent plane trees in Berkeley Square (where the nightingale sang) were planted on a mass grave of plague victims in the time of Queen Anne. The double avenue of planes on either side of the Mall is counted one of the most level arrays in Europe. The old catalpa (overleaf) in the Gray's Inn Gardens was one of the first specimens ever brought to England.

'Fleet Street, land of black and white,
Where night is day and day is night,
Where writers burn the midnight oil
And tireless printers sweat and toil
To feed the hungry printing press
That mighty megaphone which tells
Of church bells and of wedding bells
From Timbuctoo to Tunbridge Wells.
'Fleet Street, where all the buses run,
From Ludgate Hill to Kensington. . . .'

Reginald Arkell wrote that verse on the narrow street which is the entrance to the city of London, and the outlet which sends the news from London all over the world. Dr. Samuel Johnson is reputed to have eaten steak-and-kidney pudding in the pub called the Cheshire Cheese just out of the picture on the left. The steak-and-kidney pudding is still on the bill of fare.

The world of Fleet Street, like the world of journalists everywhere, is Bohemian and raffish. Beyond St. Paul's, at the top of Ludgate Hill, a more respectable note pervades. In the City proper (*left*) you meet businessmen who look the way Englishmen are supposed to look—the top hat indicates that this wearer is on visiting terms with the banks. The bowler is just regular city uniform.

Kipling wrote of the English fields that 'in drouthy middle August, when the bones of meadow show, you can trace the lines they followed sixteen hundred years ago.' He might as easily have written how eight hundred years of history are soaked into the bones of churches like this, the old Augustinian priory of St. Bartholomew the Great in Smithfield. The church as it now stands is a fragment of the great edifice the Normans built in the twelfth century. The ambulatory arches are, in fact, a Victorian reconstruction. But here is the story of the Conqueror, the rise of the monasteries, their dissolution during the Reformation, the Commonwealth, the surging energy of Victorian England; carved in stone as lasting as the marks left in the English earth of terraced vineyards, hut circles, and the furrows made when teams of oxen pulled the plough.

Here is the pleasure of gazing at living history. And, as Hilaire Belloc said, a knowledge of history 'adds to a man, giving him, as it were, a great memory of things—like a human memory, but stretched over a far longer space than that of one human life. It makes him, I do not say wise and great, but certainly in communion with wisdom and greatness.'

The camera, peering into the apse of St. Paul's, suggests that Wren, when he designed the cathedral, had a prophetic vision of the shape of architecture to come. The fluted columns might be the models for any of the office blocks shooting up like beanstalks about St. Paul's now.

The majesty of the law. Members of the judiciary and the bar proceeding up the steps of St. Paul's for a service.

The procession of the common people. Every morning and evening, it snakes across the bridges of the Thames, a concourse syphoning in and out of the heart of a city which is already overfull. Think of the buses and the office workers as the blood stream of London. Today, there are barely enough arteries to pump them through. London Bridge.

Of all the gloomy places of the world, I know only one in which the very stones seem to drip blood the way they do in the Tower of London; and that's in the old city of Jerusalem. The Tower is a monument of sorrow. It's one of the places every child is taken to see. It is unarguably one of the most historic sites of London. But it's no pleasure to a sensitive spirit with a knowledge of history. The ravens, who are on the payroll, seem the embodiment of the evil which has been done here.

Church Street which, trafficwise, is a rather puzzling gutter from Notting Hill Gate to Royal Kensington, is the junk collector's paradise. On either side of it, there's a colony of artists and discerning professional men living in discreet mews houses which you may judge from the outside are furnished inside regardless.

Down Church Street itself is a line of antique shops which are among the peripatetic charms of London. In the antique market, Church Street stands, with Chelsea, in the middle bracket. The happy hunting ground of the collector is said to be in second-hand shops in little towns outside London (I'm not at all sure that the rule is inviolable). The place where you pay, but where you can usually count on the best, is in the West End.

What every private collector should know is that the antique market is essentially a cannibalistic one. The dealers live by selling to each other. If an object goes cheap in a country house auction sale, the man on the spot will buy it in the knowledge that he can sell better to a dealer in Church Street. The man in Church Street will take it because he can make a profit by flogging it to one of the fashionable Mayfair shops. The clever private buyer is the one who can spot the bargain down the line.

None could do better than start here in the middle range. When you have got the measure of the current values in Church Street you're well on the way to recognising an unconsidered trifle in a country town, and knowing whether you're being rooked in . . . well, never mind where.

When Queen Anne was at Kensington Palace these were her private gardens. It wasn't until a little more than a hundred and fifty years ago that they began to assume the character of a public park. Even then Kensington Gardens were only open on Saturdays for a social parade of 'the ton.' It wasn't until society, in the fickle way of high society, made it more fashionable to be seen along Rotten Row in Hyde Park that the nursemaids and their charges moved in.

Then came the time when a nursemaid would pay one of those scarlet-coated footguards from Horse Guards Parade (*overleaf*) to come out walking with her there, while his officers and her mistress were perambulating along Bird Cage Walk in St. James's.

There's no recognised place for social parade in London today. Kensington Gardens and Hyde Park have both become largely exercise grounds for dogs. In the age of the motor car, the charm of walks, even in pleached walks like this, has been forgotten.

Kensington Gardens, Pleached Walk of Lime Trees

*William III
in the centre of
St. James's Square*

Don't turn a blind eye to London's sculpture. Some of it, like President Roosevelt's statue in Grosvenor Square, is awful. By contrast, Grinling Gibbons's figure of James II outside the National Gallery in Trafalgar Square is a masterpiece. Highly recommended: the equestrian bronze of George III in Cockspur Street not far away from James II; the contemporary statue of Charles I (which Cromwell thought had been melted down for cannon balls) and the statue (*opposite*) of William III in St. James's Square. To my eye, the silhouette of William III, seen from King Street against the floodlit elevation of the Haymarket Theatre, is one of the most evocative views in London.

By contrast, it's easy to laugh at Reid Dick's whimsy Peter Pan in Kensington Gardens; but it is not meant for the fastidious. Sufficient that it is the delight of children; and that is a justification in art in itself.

James Barrie's Peter Pan beside the Serpentine

Marks and Spencer's, the multiple clothing stores, have probably done more to raise the standards of good value and good taste than any other popular institution of our time. London is as well dressed as she is today—especially her children—largely through the genius of Sir Simon Marks and his colleagues in marketing clothes which are not only cheap but well designed.

To those who are snobbish about the name on the label inside their shirts or their briefs, Old Bond Street looks better; but it's becoming increasingly 'old hat.' One of the most significant changes in the social pattern of London in recent years is that people who wouldn't be seen dead in something which isn't *comme il faut* look down their superior noses at those who don't wear the St. Michael brand of smalls.

None expressed it better than the man who said: 'My wife dresses at Balenciaga, but she's all 'Marks and Sparks' underneath.

The stocking counter of M. & S. in Oxford Street

After Marks and Spencer's in Oxford Street, Fortnum and Mason's of Piccadilly. It's said that a customer here, after producing a five pound note to pay for some exotic trifle, was surprised to be offered some change. 'Keep it,' he said, 'I trod on a strawberry.'

Fortnum's isn't just another shop, it's part of a luxurious London tradition. The food counters are surely the most exciting in the world. Even the humble sardine swims in sauces as memorable as a Château Lafite. True, Fortnum's sell other things beside food; but it's the food, an Ali Baba's cave of it, which has made this a gourmet's paradise.

My father once said to me, as he explored the treasures on the cheese counter: 'Ain't Grub Grand?' Here is grub in the grand manner.

Epicure's Corner

Superior dogs, off the leash from nannies attached to pram handles, still club together in Kensington Gardens. Time was when the show place of superior horsemanship was Rotten Row in Hyde Park. It isn't now. The Sunday parade after church has passed. The turn-out of high-steppers and elegant equestrians has been succeeded by pony-tailed children learning to ride and, worse, by people in the wrong clothes who believe that they can. Today, Hyde Park is just another parking-place, where the police allow it, for cars.

On your left, the citadel of men. On your right, that part of London where women have got the edge. South of Piccadilly—you're looking at a back-view of it outside Boodle's Club—you will certainly see women, but passing modestly on their way. In Bond Street, the heart of Mayfair, you'll see men about their own affairs as well, hastening through to get a cummerbund at Gieves, a dozen shirts, an old school tie; or because they are on their way to Trumper's for a haircut. But you may assume that most men, north of Piccadilly, are about women's business.

They're late for a date with a girl at Claridge's. There's a romantic blob to be repaired with an armful of garnet roses from Constance Spry. Or perhaps it's one of those occasions when a fellow is slipping surreptitiously into Asprey's to inquire the cost of a diamond bracelet or an emerald ring.

The division between the two sides of Piccadilly is inexact, but unmistakable. In one, the Briggs umbrella and the Coke hat still rule; in the other diamonds glitter in the shop windows and nylons twinkle in the streets.

The quiet terrace sandwiched between the Mall and Pall Mall, between the flashing pin-table of Piccadilly Circus and the traffic blocks in Parliament Square. In the shadow of Nelson's column, Lord Palmerston, Mr. Gladstone and the great sporting peer, Lord Lonsdale, had their London mansions. Today, most of it is occupied by departments of the Foreign Office, with the Foreign Secretary's home just behind us at this end. At this end, too, was the home of the famous Bohemian club, the Savage; at the other, Crockford's the gaming club.

But Carlton House Terrace is changing. The soft and lovely street lamps will soon shine down, even if they're allowed to remain, on different company. The value of the property is now so great that the Crown Lands Commissioners intend to develop it for offices and penthouses for business tycoons. Unfortunately, the supply of tycoons with money to burn shows no signs of drying up. Until that happens, it seems useless to plead the cause of good taste or cultural quiet.

L ondon's green places, from the central lungs of Hyde Park, Green Park, Kensington Gardens and Regent's Park to out-lying ones like Richmond Park and Wimbledon Common, Clapham Common and Hampstead Heath, have always been one of London's prides. But all of them are progressively con-tracting. The need to deal with the increasing flow of traffic has scarred new motor roads over the bridle tracks. A growing population, and the pertinacity of building speculators, has buried more and more grass under bricks and mortar.

It isn't simply the problem of a metropolis which has grown too big and too unwieldy. It's the problem of the whole of this small and overcrowded island; perhaps the greatest problem, although it isn't widely recognised yet, that we face in the future.

There was a time, not long ago, when misguided agricultural economists prophesied that, unless population and urban expansion was retarded, we should starve. Nobody believes that now. Advances in agricultural science in Britain are such that it is confidently predicted that, before long, we can be totally self-supporting in food, however large the population grows. We've already developed seed mixtures which will ensure the growth of grass for animal feed twelve months, instead of five months, a year.

Our food supplies, from the agricultural land which is left, aren't in danger. The danger is what will happen to human beings brought up in the artificial surroundings of great cities; a sub-species which comes to believe that flagstones underfoot and skyscrapers overhead are natural; that food is something which is produced by a supermarket.

A great humanist has suggested that a time is coming when people living in cities will have to be turned out to grass, like the poor cart-horses of the past, 'to regain touch with reality again.' The trend is already showing. Increasingly, areas of Britain are being designated as National Beauty Spots and National Parks. It may not be so far away before we count places where people can play, like these children with their ponies on Wimbledon Common, our greatest treasure. We have been profligate far too long. Look over the page; you'll see what I mean.

Before the war, it was a rarity to see a coloured face in London at all. There was no colour problem because there were no coloured people. Today, negroes are as much a part of London's life as they are of any American city.

Most are Jamaicans who, as citizens of the Commonwealth, have come here for the work and wages that they can't get at home. They're glad to take the sort of jobs which, in an affluent society, native-born Londoners regard as menial. So, increasingly, the dustmen, the bus conductors, the underground porters—on a higher level the operator who comes to fix the telephone or TV—are negroes.

Inevitably, they have brought social problems with them. Because of the shortage of houses, they tend to herd together. In a new land, they seek each other's company in districts like Notting Hill Gate north of the Park. Although prejudice is surprisingly small, considering the size and novelty of the invasion, it is still there.

But the new Londoners are here to stay. Most of London has already accepted them.

In the poorer areas (*left*) where social and economic pressures have brought black and white close together, the children are sharing the same schools. So, by the time these youngsters grow up integration should be complete.

'Walking in the Zoo on Sunday is the O.K. thing to do. . . .' So sang the Victorian music hall comic. The fellows of the Zoological Gardens in Regents Park couldn't conceal their indignation. In the fifty years since the Society's foundation, nobody before had coined the inelegant word 'Zoo.' Inevitably, the apoplectic fellows lost to a vulgarism which was anyhow better than the pedantry of a name which few people could even pronounce. Today, the Oxford Dictionary defines the word 'Zoo' as 'The Zoological Gardens in London'; and, in a worthy endeavour not to seem insular, 'any similar collection of animals elsewhere.'

The London Zoo was founded in 1828 by none other than Sir Humphry Davy, then President of the Royal Society and the inventor of the miner's lamp, and Sir Stamford Raffles, who advised Britain to purchase Singapore. Because the London Zoo was one of the earliest metropolitan collections of animals it is today, by comparison with metropolitan zoos in other places, out of date; although the collection of specimens rates with any in the world. Just as London is changing, so the Zoo is changing. Not the least of its new improvements is an aviary designed by Lord Snowdon.

It's still true in London that 'walking in the Zoo is the O.K. thing to do,' although these days many people—and I number myself one of them—dislike seeing animals in captivity. Nevertheless, the contribution of the Zoological Society to the study of animals has been, and is, incomparable. For that reason alone, the cages are justified.

The greatest treasure of the Royal Zoological Society isn't in its enclosures, but in the library of books on the Society's shelves. There is no finer nor more exhaustive literature on zoology anywhere else in the world.

It has been called the Cockney's paradise, the funfair in the highlands of Hampstead Heath on August Bank Holiday. The bank holidays, as they're called, four of them in a year, are left overs from a time when holidays given to bank employees were extended to the whole nation. You can compare them, without benefit of religious fervour, to the feast days on the Continent.

Hampstead Heath, when Dick Turpin made his legendary ride to York, was very different from the untidy picture it frames on heydays and holidays now. In winter, the trellis work of the trees, the bare heath, still preserves something of the old isolation. You can believe in a time, not so long ago, when it was a brave man, in a nest of footpads and highwaymen, who rode alone.

A contributor to *Punch* wrote the couplet: '*The policeman with uplifted hand conducts the vast orchestral Strand.*'

But it's an orchestra of traffic which plays in fits and starts, forever tuning up rather than following the policeman's hand in a concerted movement. The historic churches of St. Mary le Strand, in the foreground, and, behind, St. Clement Danes, are ringed with a cacophony of noise. It's a bold spirit these days who ventures through the traffic to reach them. But it's worth it. There's quiet inside.

Charles Dickens's parents were married in St. Mary le Strand. It was the bells of St. Clement's which sang 'Oranges and Lemons.' At the back of St. Clement's, in a sad little patch of grass in the midst of the paving stones and the tarmac, is the statue of Dr. Samuel Johnson, the lexicographer, who said that 'if a man is tired of London, he is tired of life.' He looks down Fleet Street where, for so long, he lived and worked. But if anybody tells you that it was Johnson who also said 'Sir, let us take a walk down Fleet Street,' deny it. Johnson never did. It's a piece of apocrypha which even that meticulous student of detail, Kipling, was taken in by. In fact, the phrase was invented by the Victorian journalist, George Augustus Sala.

The Strand, so-called because it was once literally the strand of London's river before the Thames was dammed back by a succession of embankments, is still rich in association with the time when this was the main highway from the city's Ludgate to the open country. Today, the two lovely churches isolated in the traffic are about all that's left of more leisurely times. But in the little courts and back streets adjoining the old highway, there are still remnants which the inquisitive wanderer can uncover.

The Fleet River, which was so malodorous that even Dr. Johnson had to hold his nose when he crossed it into the city, still runs down the road under Farringdon Street and New Bridge Street. Now it is officially a main sewer. You can see it trickling into the Thames under Blackfriars Bridge.

Those were coachmen's quarters (*on the left*) in the times when the well-to-do lived in mansions behind the mews, and only those who couldn't afford to live on the fashionable side of the park occupied houses on the banks of the Regent's Canal. Not now. In the tide of fashion, the rich have moved out of big houses with no servants into little houses where servants used to live. The newcomers to the banks of the Regent's Canal have given the area a social cachet by naming it 'Little Venice.'

In a nationally popular radio programme, a famous and much-beloved countryman said that, every time he passed through Trafalgar Square, the sight of the pigeons made him sick. As a farmer he knew what an unmitigated pest they are to crops. Overnight he became as unpopular with city dwellers as the man who expressed his disgust that the mob of pigeons in St. Mark's Square should be fed at public expense while so many human Venetians are starving. Londoners, like the citizens of so many other capitals, just love pigeons.

Never mind that the damage the birds do by dropping their lime on public buildings and monuments costs hundreds of thousands of pounds a year to clean and repair. Never mind that the birds, many of them the descendants of escapees from the monastic columbaries where they were bred for food, and traps from which in the past they were released to be shot for 'sport,' are many of them infected with avian tuberculosis. To the Londoners, who delight in feeding them and having their pictures taken with a pigeon sitting on their hands, the birds are sacrosanct. The licensed photographers and the vendors of bags of dried peas make a good thing out of it.

As a consequence, the Ministry of Works is forced to combat the pigeons' missile attacks on public property with discreet circumspection. It happens that London has been the first city in the world to find a way to shoo them off where they are not wanted. The secret is to dress the ledges of buildings where pigeons roost with a soft substance resistant to weather which gives them a sense of insecurity when they land. It doesn't do them any harm, but they fly off.

The fountains in Trafalgar Square are one of the sights of the town. They are ordinary enough by comparison with the fountains in most continental cities; but, in London, fountains have a rarity value. There are so surprisingly few of them. Eros in Piccadilly Circus has a fountain; but it has never worked properly. So Londoners come here.

It's odd how few of them ever journey further east to look at the magic of London's greatest watercourse.

'*The sun comes up like thunder on the road to Mandalay,*
But it creeps up on you quietlike downriver Limehouse way.
Though Bugsby's Reach throws up the scent of bone and manure, and glue,
The sky dove grey and lemon warms to topaz shot with blue. . . .'

So the parodist of Kipling's poem. Every lounger under a street lamp knows those grey and lemon dawns. Surprisingly few, except those who live in the area, could tell you where Bugsby's Reach is. Most Cockneys are only half aware that this old city is also one of the greatest ports of the world.

In New York, the great ships ride into Manhattan. In Southampton, you are aware of their majestic presence all over town. In Hamburg, the berths seem to occupy more spàce than the city. In London, it's quite a ride just to find your way through the traffic to the docks. Many never see them.

Yet we live on one of the most crowded and exciting waterways in the world, a waterway almost too small for the tonnage which uses it and discharges its cargoes into the warehouses on Thames-side. The mud pilots, who bring the ocean-going ships into the Pool, have to ease them in with inches to spare on either side.

Turn the page, and look what goes on east of the Tower. . . .

Shoppers in the East End. A generation ago, the gulf between the East and West Ends was as wide as the difference between the gallery and the stalls. It's less noticeable now; but the East Enders remain more demonstrative, closer to life on the streets, readier to leave off their ties and roll up their sleeves.

Among the shoppers in the West End, you miss the warmth (don't you?) of the opposite picture. Here, everybody is busy minding their own business; in this weather, largely a matter of dodging the spikes of other people's umbrellas. There are no street-traders, no barrow boys shouting their wares. The crowds are strangely anonymous.

They know nothing of life who can't guess the improbable comedies and tragedies played out behind windows like this—in London, hundreds of miles of them. To a motorist, driving into the city, the view seems endlessly anonymous, even monotonous; the little houses, the twisted chimneys, the patterned curtains and the locked doors. But it is behind such windows that murders are committed, that geniuses are born, and that too many people experience ineffable loneliness. It isn't peculiar to London.

Here, in one superb photograph, is the war between the old and the new; a mediaeval arch, within a hairsbreadth of the old London wall, and one of the centrally-heated, air-conditioned boot-box office blocks which are raising their heads in London now.

There are those of us who feel that this city is now becoming a cheque book playground; a place which, with all its faults, is still one of the greatest cities in the world. The tragedy of the things which are being put up now is that they not only lack charm—dwarfing the decent buildings about them—but they are monoliths of human servitude. How nice it would be if London looked again to its old stones! How much happier its people would be if this city was smaller, if it wasn't necessary to fight into a concrete wilderness to work!

The Season, which begins with the opening of the Royal Academy in May and extends to Royal Goodwood in the autumn, traditionally marks the start and finish of London's social round. Between times, except for occasional sorties to the capital for charity balls and what not, the gentry are theoretically supposed to rusticate. It's a hangover from a time when, from the turning of the leaf to the sowing of the spring wheat, everybody who was anybody was supposed to be fully engaged shooting the grouse moors, partridge manors and pheasant coverts; and catching foxes in the shires. In practice, even top people these days have to work for a living. But the nostalgia for a time when, in Disraeli's words, the world was 'the few and the very few' remains.

The annual match between Eton and Harrow at Lords, in which scarcely anybody bothers to watch the cricket—and who can blame them on an occasion when chaps' daughters and sisters are on parade?—is just one of the events in which morning coats and grey toppers, which can be hired for a very reasonable charge from Messrs. Moss Bros., are still worn.

But the men take second place to the women at the Chelsea Flower Show (*right*). Only some of the flowers are in the marquee.

The street markets of London—this one in the Portobello Road is held every Saturday—are survivals of a time when all trading was carried on in the streets. The contemporary shop is a comparatively recent innovation, not much earlier than the beginning of the eighteenth century. The traders in the traditional markets, mostly selling second-hand goods, are clinging to rights granted in most cases hundreds of years ago. They interfere with the traffic, even the passage of pedestrians, but they remain immensely popular.

Most people go to them sooner or later in the hope of a bargain. Many enjoy the oriental haggling over a price, because anybody who pays what they're originally asked for here is a muggins.

The remnant markets of London are essentially remnants themselves of an earlier way of going shopping. Overleaf is a new aspect of London which, until recently, no photographer could achieve. It's been taken from the top of Shell's new skyscraper building. On the other side of the river, which somebody has described as 'liquid history,' is the terrace of the Houses of Parliament where, in summer time, the M.P.'s entertain their friends to strawberry-and-cream teas. Now try naming the bridges.

I remember asking a small boy who was fishing for tiddlers in one of the London parks whether he had had any sport. Showing me an empty jamjar, he chucked a thumb at a party of children playing with toy yachts. 'That's why,' he said bitterly, 'it's those bloody boats.'

It was the excuse of a true fisherman. And I couldn't help feeling sad that there isn't more space for the budding anglers and the budding yachtsmen to exercise their skills. You've only got to walk along the Serpentine, or the Round Pond on a summer's day, to see how far room to play falls short of demand.

Before New York claimed the title of being the largest city in the world, London wore the uneasy crown. I would be happy to think that London was half its present size, and had twice as much of this.

It might be a backdrop out of 'The Mikado', or a film set for the fleeing lovers in the story of the Willow Pattern Plate. In fact, it's one of the more improbable views of London on the way from Hampstead to Oxford Street. The wooden bridge over the Regent's Canal was the gift of a philanthropist who was in love with Regent's Park.

But, personally, I like this picture for the sparrows lined up here like a chorus in a night club before the curtain. If Cockneys chose a symbol for themselves it would surely be the sparrow, the pert brown bird of the London streets. To be exact, the sparrow is probably, with its enemy the cat, one of the most cosmopolitan creatures in the world. I found a colony of them quite at home on an uninhabited island in the Indian Ocean. But London has identified herself with the species.

At a time when one of the civic problems was the daily collection of hundreds of tons of horse manure, the London sparrows proliferated and grew fat on the proceeds. Today, there are not so many of them. But the remainder can boast that they are descendants of the sparrows who feasted on the droppings of the Iron Duke's horse.

How decorative a girl can instinctively make herself. This one
is ornamenting magnolia time in the Royal Botanical Gardens
at Kew.

How difficult it is for adolescent young men not to look like
blots on the landscape. Two youths in Battersea Park.

Many a Londoner born within sound of Bow Bells has never been inside Westminster Abbey. There may well be Romans who have never entered St. Peter's, or Parisians the cathedral of Notre Dame. It's a human failing to overlook things within daily reach that other people cross the world to see.

Yet this is the shrine of Britain, 'a fabric built up of architectural grandeur, of traditional worship, and of the inescapable and immemorial presence of ourselves and our ancestors.'

There are few bastions in London which are more resistant to change or cling harder to traditional practices, than the markets of Covent Garden (for fruit and vegetables, *left*), Smithfield (for meat) and Billingsgate (for fish). To the outsider they are scenes of Cockney chaos in which the traffic is seemingly always inextricably jammed, in which everybody is precariously balancing a load or using a barrow like a battering ram, and the market produce sprawls higgledy-piggledy over the road. But let anybody suggest, bold spirits sometimes do, that the markets should be moved to more convenient and commodious premises, and there's an outcry from the very men who have to put up with the discomfort of the present ones.

The Billingsgate fish porters, whose name has become synonymous with foul language, would no more part with their wooden hats (for carrying fish on) than lose the reputation of their tongues.

Automation, in the markets where the pubs open at 5 in the morning and men eat steaks for breakfast, is a very dirty word.

The lamp might be the dial of a City of London policeman—you can always recognise the City of London force because they have centurion's crests on their helmets—who, more in sorrow than in anger, has caught you driving on the right of the road; and with St. Paul's looking on, too. It's a photograph as good as any to deal with a question which visitors to Britain so often ask. Why do we drive on the left?

The sixty-four thousand dollar question, to those of you who come from the Americas or the Continent, is what on earth persuaded you people to change to the right?

Think on it. When roads were more dangerous, in a different sense from the way they are now, the traveller always took care to keep close to the left. The reason was that, if he was attacked, he had a space on his right side to defend himself with his sword or his pistol. The tradition is so deeply ingrained that, to this day, no man would dream of leading his bride to the altar with her arm leaning on other than his left side. It is still counted a matter of manners for a man to escort a woman on his left along the street. In the days of duelling, it was considered just occasion for a challenge if a passer-by cut in on the inside of a lady.

So don't ask why we drive on the left of the road. We are simply observing a sense of historic propriety. What I have never discovered is who thought it was a good notion to change to the right. Was it the man who was defeated at the Battle of Waterloo?

Here's British colonialism for you; an African calling down hell and high water, maybe, on wicked imperialists. And good luck to him. He has the most tolerant audience and the most liberal platform on earth. He's giving the works from his soapbox in Hyde Park.

Here is one of the most precious traditions of Parliamentary democracy, the right of any man to speak his mind without fear, providing only that he doesn't preach the overthrow of the constitution. About the Government, religion, any personal bee in his bonnet, he is welcome to say what he likes.

It's not that the British system is more amiable than others; but, rather, subtler. Nothing is more dangerous than a minority smothered into a conspiracy. The corners of London, there are others traditionally recognised, where anybody who is in the mood can blow his top until he's hoarse, provide the safety valve which any healthy society needs.

It also gives a regular entertainment for the audiences, too; an opportunity for the hecklers to exercise their wits. As the regular speakers are inclined to be repetitive and many of the audience are regular customers, question and answers often have the familiarity of a well rehearsed music-hall act.

Many years ago, there was a regular speaker with a grudge about everything who was so popular that his audience subscribed to buy him a speaker's rostrum, and made a collection whenever he appeared so that he could wet his whistle when his eloquence was exhausted.

THE END

A glimpse of a young art lover at a street gallery at Hampstead.